World Wisdom
The Library of Perennial Philosophy

The Library of Perennial Philosophy is ... e timeless Truth underlying the diverse religio ... as the *Sophia Perennis*—or Perennial Wisdom— ... ed Scriptures as well as the writings of the great sages and ... of the traditional worlds.

Spirit of the Earth: Indian Voices on Nature appears as one of our selections in the Sacred Worlds series.

Sacred Worlds Series

The Sacred Worlds series blends images of visual beauty with focused selections from the writings of the great religions of the world, including both scripture and the writings of the sages and saints. Books in the Sacred Worlds series may be based upon a particular religious tradition, or upon a universal religious theme such as prayer or virtue.

Praise for the Sacred Worlds Series

"[This series] combines impressive imagery—both new and old fine arts, as well as contemporary and vintage photography—with selections from world faith traditions. . . . These entries in the 'Sacred Worlds' series are delights to the eye and the mind."

—Library Journal

Encampment of Blackfoot Confederation,
near Gleichen, Alberta, c. 1900

About the Editors

"One of the great callings of art is to excavate a lost part of our culture, and the Fitzgeralds answer this summons handsomely here in a compact exploration of Native American women's spirituality."
　　—Publishers Weekly on *The Spirit of Indian Women*

"*The Spirit of Indian Women* . . . is an act of reclamation as much as of spirituality: it reproduces precious and seldom-seen photographs of Native American women, most of them from the later 19th century. Their images are interwoven with oral accounts, songs, and other documents that offer priceless glimpses into the little-understood lives and experiences of America's foremothers. . . . *The Spirit of Indian Women* is a special treasure. Highly recomended."
　　—Library Journal

"This new World Wisdom version of [*World of the Teton Sioux Indians*] . . . is effectively edited by Joseph A. Fitzgerald to facilitate its reading and allow the lay reader to enjoy the discovery, depth, and meaning of tribal culture and the songs that were handed down from time immemorial."
　　—Charles Trimble, former Executive Director of the American Indian Press Association, author of *Iyeska*

"Michael Fitzgerald has heard the poignant narratives of the American Indian people, and has lived among the Crow people for extended periods of time since 1970. He has studied American Indian religious traditions on the earth, among the people, in ceremonies and family gatherings. We thank Fitzgerald for his deep-seated appreciation, honor, and respect for American Indian culture, its religion, language, and lifeways."
　　—Janine Pease, founding president of the Little Big Horn College, and National Indian Educator of the Year

"My son, Michael Fitzgerald, has been a member of my family and the Crow tribe for over twenty years. Michael has helped to preserve the spiritual traditions of the Crow Sun Dance and he has helped to show us the wisdom of the old-timers."
　　—Thomas Yellowtail, Crow Medicine Man and Sun Dance Chief

"I greatly appreciate the recovery work that Fitzgerald is doing, work that makes available for the classroom and popular use texts that have been all but buried in libraries. Work such as Fitzgerald's is exactly the kind of work that needs to be promoted for a more complete understanding of early American Indian writings and oratory."
　　—Stephen Brandon, University of New Mexico

SPIRIT OF THE EARTH

INDIAN VOICES ON NATURE

Edited by

MICHAEL OREN FITZGERALD
&
JOSEPH A. FITZGERALD

Foreword by

JOSEPH BRUCHAC

World Wisdom

Spirit of the Earth: Indian Voices on Nature
© 2017 World Wisdom, Inc.

Library of Congress Cataloging-in-Publication Data

Names: Fitzgerald, Michael Oren, 1949- editor. | Fitzgerald, Joseph A., 1977-
editor.
Title: Spirit of the earth : Indian voices on nature / edited by Michael Oren
Fitzgerald & Joseph A. Fitzgerald ; foreword by Joseph Bruchac.
Other titles: Indian voices on nature
Description: Bloomington, IN : World Wisdom, [2017] | Series: Sacred worlds
series | Includes bibliographical references and index.
Identifiers: LCCN 2016049476 (print) | LCCN 2016049870 (ebook) | ISBN
9781936597543 (pbk. : alk. paper) | ISBN 9781936597550 (epub)
Subjects: LCSH: Indian philosophy–North America. | Indians of North
America–Quotations. | Nature photography–United States. | Philosophy of
nature.
Classification: LCC E98.P5 S65 2017 (print) | LCC E98.P5 (ebook) | DDC
970.004/97–dc23
LC record available at https://lccn.loc.gov/2016049476

Front cover: Maroon Bells-Snowmass Wilderness,
White River National Forest, Colorado. Photo by unknown.

Back cover: Blackfeet Reservation, Montana, c. 1910.
Photo by Edward S. Curtis.

Printed on acid-free paper in China.

For information address World Wisdom, Inc.
P.O. Box 2682, Bloomington, Indiana 47402-2682
www.worldwisdom.com

MITAKUYE
OYASIN

"WE ARE
ALL RELATED"

CONTENTS

INDIAN VOICES   1

Harvested
flint corn

FOREWORD

We human beings are not apart from nature. We are in nature. We have always been and always will be part of nature. I've heard or read such words time and time again, words spoken by elders—past and present—from virtually all our different American Indian nations.

It's reflected in the way our indigenous languages work. As Chester Nez, one of the twenty-nine Navajo men who created the unbroken Navajo code used in World War II expressed it in his 2011 autobiography *Code Talker*, "Our language illustrates [our] relationship to nature."

In a conversation we had a few years ago, Tom Sakonienkwas Porter, a Mohawk elder, illustrated that relationship by explaining that "In our language we would not say something is blue. We would say it is the color of the sky."

That connection—which is not merely linguistic but also spiritual—is further exemplified by our interactions with the other living things around us, even when we take their lives to support our own human existence. Among my own Abenaki people, when we catch a fish, the proper thing to say to it is, "May you continue to swim." When we kill a game animal, we say, "May you continue to run"; when we harvest a plant, "May you continue to grow."

Our lives are connected to everything around us in the natural world, not above the rest of existence, but woven into it. It is just such a weaving together of our human existence and of all life around us—like threads in one blanket—that is beautifully presented to us by this collection of images and voices from a great variety of North American Indian people.

There are a number of things that strike me about this luminous collection, things that distinguish it from most other collections of photos of American Indians paired with quotations. First of all, most of the images were not chosen from Edward S. Curtis' rightly famous *The North American Indian*. Curtis' effective, intentionally romantic style was designed to make his subjects look as authentic as possible. (Curtis carried with him a trunk filled with wigs and regalia to insure that his often short-haired subjects looked more appropriately Indian.) There are, indeed, sixteen of Curtis' wonderful photographs among the over sixty pictures, but they in no way dominate the landscape.

In fact, and this is the second reason the collection stands out, the landscape itself is as much a focus as is any human face. Again and again—as in a two page spread showing the Valley of the Chiefs on the Crow Reservation in Montana—we are shown the land itself empty of any visible presence of people. It reminds me of something I've heard said often by my own elders and teachers, such as Maurice Dennis/Mdawelasis of the Abenaki Nation. This land was here before us and will be here after we have gone. That exact understanding is expressed in the book by the quote from one of the Omaha Warrior Societies on p. 15:

> I shall vanish and be no more,
> But the land over which I now roam
> Shall remain and change not.

And the fact that the quote is paired with a marvelous winter photo of bristlecone pines—among the oldest living trees on earth—makes it even more striking.

Thinking of those beings who were here before us, the animals and birds themselves are also pictured again and again on their own. An eagle sweeping across the sky, a bull elk bugling. That our non-human brothers and sisters are acknowledged and honored in this way is a third reason for my liking this volume so much.

Then, there are the quotations themselves. So well chosen, so well paired with the images, and so beautifully centered on our appreciation, understanding, and lasting reliance on the natural world, they do what our traditional stories have always done—engage and teach. They also span the four directions, drawn from nearly fifty different tribal nations, ranging from our Algonquin and Iroquoian peoples of the northeast Atlantic Coast to the maritime nations of the Pacific coast.

There is more that I could say, but a good introduction should be just that. It should, like the traditional Thanksgiving Address my Haudenosaunee (Iroquois) friends and teachers speak at the start of every gathering, simply set the stage, remind us to greet and thank all the aspects of Creation, and then step aside.

As I do now. *Wlipamkaani*—Enjoy the journey.

— Joseph Bruchac

PREFACE

Often spoken at the end of a prayer, a well-known Sioux phrase affirms that "we are all related" (*mitakuye oyasin*).[1] Similarly, the Sioux medicine man, Brave Buffalo, came to realize when he was still a boy that "the maker of all was Wakan Tanka, and . . . in order to honor him I must honor his works in nature" (see p. 63). The interconnectedness of all things, and the respect all things are due, are among the most prominent—and most welcome—themes in this collection of Indian voices on nature.[2]

The native peoples of North America did not, as most of us do today, observe the natural world from afar or experience a tamed version of it in parks or backyards; they lived in and from nature during every moment of life. Their relationship with nature thus necessarily touched on all dimensions of the human condition, from the practical to the spiritual and every aspect in between. It included the sentiments, but could not remain merely sentimental, as can our largely distant and abstract relationship with nature today. And no one who looks at the state of the world can deny the bitter fruits that this scission between humanity and nature has borne.

"[T]here are many different ways of seeing the world and expressing the wisdom of Native beliefs," writes Joseph Bruchac. "No one voice speaks for all voices, though some things are largely held in common. . . ."[3] We have tried for this reason to be as inclusive as possible by presenting quotations from men and women of nearly fifty North American tribes.[4] Most of these speakers were born and reared in the eighteenth or

1 This phrase can also be translated as "all my relatives" or "all my relations."

2   Frithjof Schuon describes these two themes as the "consciousness of the profound homogeneity of the created world and the sense of universal solidarity which results therefrom. All creatures, including plants and even minerals—and likewise things in Nature, such as stars or wind—are brother; everything is animate, and each thing depends in a certain manner on all the others" (*The Feathered Sun: Plains Indians in Art and Philosophy* [Bloomington, IN: World Wisdom Books, 1990], p. 20).

3 *Native Wisdom* (San Francisco: Harper, 1995), p. 4.

4 We have in most cases used conventional names and spellings for individual speakers and their tribes. We have generally not noted tribal sub-divisions, but we have occasionally made reference in square brackets to larger groupings of tribes.

Spring Dogwoods, Hoosier National Forest, Indiana

nineteenth century, while the youngest speaker was born by 1915. All of them had lived lives intimately connected with nature and thus knew well whereof they spoke. Their legacy lives on today in contemporary Native American appreciation of the natural environment and advocacy on its behalf (see for example the Contemporary Voices at p. 106).

In an attempt to be as accurate as possible, we have checked all quotations against original written sources. This process has obliged us to omit some statements—often unattributed "proverbs" or "sayings"—whose provenance we could not establish with some degree of certainty. An extensive list of sources consulted is provided at the end the book.

We have included a photographic selection of scenes from the plains, forests, mountains, canyons, hills, deserts, swamps, and shores of what today is the United States and Canada. These images are meant to indicate, in keeping with the wide range of native voices, something of the diversity of the North American natural world. We have included in addition a number of historical photographs of American Indians

and their material culture. These show a life in nature that undeniably included difficulty but which was considered as both meaningful and beautiful by those who lived it. In the words of a Navajo song of the Night Chant:

> In beauty I walk.
> With beauty before me, I walk.
> With beauty behind me, I walk.
> With beauty below me, I walk.
> With beauty above me, I walk.
> With beauty all around me, I walk.
> It is finished in beauty.

Our goal here is to present in beauty something of nature's timeless message as described through Indian voices.

— Michael Oren Fitzgerald & Joseph A. Fitzgerald

INDIAN VOICES

*Joshua trees in Antelope Valley
(Mojave Desert), California*

INDIAN VOICES

DID YOU KNOW THAT trees talk? Well they do. They talk to each other, and they'll talk to you if you listen. . . . I have learned a lot from trees: sometimes about the weather, sometimes about animals, sometimes about the Great Spirit.

Walking Buffalo (Tatanka-mani), Stoney

WE DO NOT LIKE TO harm the trees. Whenever we can, we always make an offering of tobacco to the trees before we cut them down. We never waste the wood, but use all that we cut down. If we did not think of their feelings, and did not offer them tobacco before cutting them down, all the other trees in the forest would weep, and that would make our hearts sad, too.

Unidentified Mesquakie

Moss, duckweed, and cypress
trees in Caddo Lake, Texas

INDIAN VOICES

LOOK AT ME MY FRIEND! I come to ask you for your dress, for you have come to take pity on us; for there is nothing for which you cannot be used. . . . I came to beg you for this . . . for I am going to make a basket for lily root out of you. I pray you, friend, not to feel angry with me on account of what I am going to do to you; and I beg you, friend, to tell our friends about what I ask of you. Take care, friend!

Unidentified Kwakiutl, addressing a cedar tree

ᑕᑕᑕ

PERHAPS YOU HAVE NOTICED that even in the very lightest breeze you can hear the voice of the cottonwood tree: this we understand is its prayer to the Great Spirit, for not only men, but all things and all beings pray to Him continually in differing ways.

Black Elk (Hehaka-sapa), Sioux

ᑕᑕᑕ

THE LAKOTA WAS A TRUE naturist—a lover of nature. He loved the earth and all things of the earth, the attachment growing with age. The old people came literally to love the soil and they sat or reclined on the ground with a feeling of being close to a mothering power. It was good for the skin to touch the earth and the old people liked to remove their moccasins and walk with bare feet on the sacred earth. Their tipis were built upon the earth and their altars were made of earth. The birds that flew in the air came to rest upon the earth and it was the final abiding place of all things that lived and grew. The soil was soothing, strengthening, cleansing, and healing.

That is why the old Indian still sits upon the earth instead of propping himself up and away from its life-giving forces. For him, to sit or lie upon the ground is to be able to think more deeply and to feel more keenly; he can see more clearly into the mysteries of life and come closer in kinship to other lives about him.

Luther Standing Bear, Sioux

INDIAN VOICES

You ask me to plow the ground. Shall I take a knife and tear my mother's bosom? Then when I die she will not take me to her bosom to rest.

You ask me to dig for stone. Shall I dig under her skin for bones? Then when I die I cannot enter her body to be born again.

You ask me to cut grass and make hay and sell it, and be rich like white men. But how dare I cut off my mother's hair?

Smohalla, Wanapum

You say: "Why do not the Indians till the ground and live as we do?" May we not ask with equal propriety, "Why do not the white people hunt and live as we do?"

Old Tassel, Cherokee

Lupines in Canoe Landing Prairie State Natural Area, Wisconsin

INDIAN VOICES

Wife of Turkey Legs (Cheyenne), preparing a cowhide, near Busby, Montana, c. 1925

THE ANIMALS LONG AGO agreed to sacrifice their lives for ours, when we are in need of food or of skins for garments, but we are forbidden to kill for sport alone.

Ohiyesa (Charles Eastman), Sioux

I WANT TO LIVE HUMBLY, as close to the earth as I can. Close to the plants, the weeds, the flowers that I use for medicine. . . . The Great Spirit made the flowers, the streams, the pines, the cedars—takes care of them. He lets a breeze go through there, makes them breathe it, waters them, makes them grow. . . . He takes care of me, waters me, feeds me, makes me live with the plants and animals as one of them.

Pete Catches, Sioux

WE RETURN THANKS TO OUR mother, the earth, which sustains us. We thank thee that thou hast caused her to yield so plentifully of her fruits. Cause that, in the season coming, she may not withhold of her fullness, and leave any to suffer for want.

We return thanks to the rivers and streams, which run their courses upon the bosom of our mother the earth. We thank thee that thou hast supplied them with life, for our comfort and support. Grant that this blessing may continue.

We return thanks to all the herbs and plants of the earth. We thank thee that in thy goodness thou hast blest them all, and given them strength to preserve our bodies healthy, and to cure us of the diseases inflicted upon us by evil spirits. We ask thee not to take from us these blessings.

Sosehawa, Seneca (Iroquois)

[E]VERYTHING ON THE EARTH has a purpose, every disease an herb to cure it, and every person a mission. This is the Indian theory of existence.

Mourning Dove (Christine Quintasket), Okanogan

Unknown Tewa, from Nambe
Pueblo, New Mexico, c. 1927

Yucca in White Sands National Park, New Mexico

INDIAN VOICES

THE EARTH HEARS YOU, THE sky and wood-mountain see
you. If you will believe this you will grow old.

Unidentified Luiseño

I WONDER IF THE GROUND HAS anything to say? I wonder
if the ground is listening to what is said? I wonder if the
ground would come alive and what is on it? Though I hear
what the ground says. The ground says, "It is the Great
Spirit that placed me here." The Great Spirit tells me to take
care of the Indians, to feed them aright. The Great Spirit
appointed the roots to feed the Indians on. The water
says the same thing. The Great Spirit directs me, "Feed the
Indians well." The grass says the same thing, "Feed the
Indians well." The ground, water, and grass say, "The Great
Spirit has given us our names. We have these names and
hold these names." The ground says, "The Great Spirit has
placed me here to produce all that grows on me, trees and
fruit." The same way the ground says, "It was from me man
was made." The Great Spirit, in placing men on the earth,
desired them to take good care of the ground and to do
each other no harm.

Young Chief, Cayuse

INDIAN VOICES

TODAY WE ARE BLESSED WITH this beautiful baby. May his feet be to the east; his right hand to the south; his head to the west; his left hand to the north. May he walk and dwell on Mother Earth peacefully.

Tom Ration, Navajo

ссс

HO! YE SUN, MOON, STARS, all ye that move in the heavens, I bid you hear me! Into your midst has come a new life. Consent ye, I implore! Make its path smooth, that it may reach the brow of the first hill!

Ho! Ye Winds, Clouds, Rain, Mist, all ye that move in the air, I bid you hear me! Into your midst has come a new life. Consent ye, I implore! Make its path smooth, that it may reach the brow of the second hill!

Ho! Ye Hills, Valleys, Rivers, Lakes, Trees, Grasses, all ye of the earth, I bid you hear me! Into your midst has come a new life. Consent ye, I implore! Make its path smooth, that it may reach the brow of the third hill!

Ho! Ye Birds, great and small, that fly in the air, Ho! Ye Animals, great and small, that dwell in the forest, Ho! Ye Insects that creep among the grasses and burrow in the ground—I bid you hear me! Into your midst has come a new life. Consent ye, I implore! Make its path smooth, that it may reach the brow of the fourth hill!

Ho! All ye of the heavens, all ye of the air, all ye of the earth; I bid you all to hear me! Into your midst has come a new life. Consent ye, consent ye all, I implore! Make its path smooth— then shall it travel beyond the four hills!

Unidentified Omaha

INDIAN VOICES

Cheyenne children, near Lame Deer, Montana, c. 1910

Balsam Lake Mountain Wild Forest
(Catskill Mountains), New York

THE EARTH IS YOUR GRANDMOTHER and mother, and she
is sacred. Every step that is taken upon her should be as a
prayer.

Black Elk (Hehaka-sapa), Sioux

GOD SAID HE WAS THE FATHER and the earth was the mother
of mankind; that nature was the law; that the animals, and
fish, and plants obeyed nature, and that man only was sinful.
This is the old law.

Smohalla, Wanapum

12

OH OUR MOTHER THE EARTH, oh our Father the Sky,
Your children are we, and with tired backs
We bring you the gifts you love.
Then weave for us a garment of brightness;
May the warp be the white light of morning,
May the weft be the red light of evening,
May the fringes be the falling rain,
May the border be the standing rainbow.
Thus weave for us a garment of brightness
That we may walk fittingly where birds sing,
That we may walk fittingly where grass is green,
Oh our Mother the Earth, oh our Father the Sky!

Song of the Sky Loom, Tewa (Pueblo)

Ancient Bristlecone
Pine Forest, Inyo National
Forest (White Mountains),
California

INDIAN VOICES

I SHALL VANISH AND BE NO MORE,
But the land over which I now roam
Shall remain and change not.

Song of the Hethushka Warrior Society,
Omaha

THERE WERE NO TEMPLES OR SHRINES
among us save those of nature. Being
a natural man, the Indian was intensely
poetical. He would deem it sacrilege to
build a house for Him who may be met
face to face in the mysterious, shadowy
aisles of the primeval forest, or on the
sunlit bosom of virgin prairies, upon
dizzy spires and pinnacles of naked rock,
and yonder in the jeweled vault of the
night sky! He who enrobes Himself in
filmy veils of cloud, there on the rim
of the visible world where our Great-
Grandfather Sun kindles his evening
campfire, He who rides upon the
rigorous wind of the north, or breathes
forth His spirit upon aromatic southern
airs, whose war-canoe is launched upon
majestic rivers and inland seas—He
needs no lesser cathedral!

Ohiyesa (Charles Eastman), Sioux

INDIAN VOICES

IN MY OPINION, IT WAS CHIEFLY owing to their deep contemplation in their silent retreats in the days of youth that the old Indian orators acquired the habit of carefully arranging their thoughts. . . . [T]he grandeur and the beauties of the forest, the majestic clouds, which appear like mountains of granite floating in the air, the golden tints of a summer evening sky, and all the changes of nature, possessed then a mysterious significance, [and] combined to furnish ample matter for reflection to the contemplating youth.

Francis Assikinack, Ojibwa

WE RETURN THANKS TO THE MOON and stars, which give us light when the sun has gone to his rest. We thank thee, that thy wisdom has so kindly provided, that light is never wanting to us. Continue unto us this goodness.

We return thanks to the sun, that he has looked upon the earth with a beneficent eye. We thank thee that thou hast, in thy unbounded wisdom, commanded the sun to regulate the return of the seasons, to dispense heat and cold, and to watch over the comfort of thy people. Give unto us that wisdom which will guide us in the path of truth. Keep us from all evil ways, that the sun may never hide his face from us for shame and leave us in darkness.

Sosehawa, Seneca (Iroquois)

INDIAN VOICES

*First Landing State Park
(Cape Henry), Virginia*

White Deer Skin Dance of the Hupa,
in Hoopa Valley, California, c. 1900.

INDIAN VOICES

THE SKY BLESSES ME; THE EARTH blesses me.
Up in the skies I cause the spirits to dance.
On the earth, the people I cause to dance.

Personal Song of Fine Day (Kamiokisihkwew), Cree

THE EARTH IS LOOKING AT ME; she is looking up at me
I am looking down on her
I am happy, she is looking at me
I am happy, I am looking at her.

The Sun is looking at me; he is looking down on me
I am looking up at him
I am happy, he is looking at me
I am happy, I am looking at him.

The Black Sky is looking at me; he is looking down on me
I am looking up at him
I am happy, he is looking at me
I am happy, I am looking at him.

The Moon is looking at me; he is looking down on me
I am looking up at him
I am happy, he is looking at me
I am happy, I am looking at him.

Song of the Creation, Navajo

INDIAN VOICES

WE ARE THANKFUL TO THE EAST because everyone feels good in the morning when they awake, and sees the bright light coming from the East, and when the Sun goes down in the West we feel good and glad we are well; then we are thankful to the West. And we are thankful to the North, because when the cold winds come we are glad to have lived to see the leaves fall again; and to the South, for when the south wind blows and everything is coming up in the spring, we are glad to live to see the grass growing and everything green again. We thank the Thunders, for they are the spirits (*manitous*) that bring the rain, which the Creator has given them power to rule over. And we thank our mother, the Earth, whom we claim as mother because the Earth carries us and everything we need. When we eat and drink and look around, we know it is Our Creator that makes us feel good that way. He gives us the purest thoughts that can be had. We should pray to Him every morning.

Charlie Elkhair, Lenape

Bluestone State Park,
West Virginia

Unknown Sioux on Pine Ridge Reservation, South Dakota, c. 1907

INDIAN VOICES

HOW PRETTY THEY ARE COMING.
The raingods make a sound up above.
How pretty! How pretty! That is so.
That is why this year the raingods will travel.
How pretty! That is so.
That is why this year the rain will fall.
How pretty! That is so.

Song to Grind Corn, Isleta (Pueblo)

YOU, WHOSE DAY IT IS, MAKE it beautiful.
Get out your rainbow colors, so it will be beautiful.

Song to Bring Fair Weather, Nootka

Quaking aspens in Sawtooth
National Recreation Area, Idaho

INDIAN VOICES

WE CALL TO MOTHER EARTH, who . . . has been asleep and resting during the night. We ask her to awake, to move, to arise, for the signs of the dawn are seen in the east and the breath of the new life is here. . . . Mother Earth hears the call; she moves, she awakes, she arises, she feels the breath of the new-born dawn. The leaves and the grass stir; all things move with the breath of the new day; everywhere life is renewed.

This is very mysterious; we are speaking of something very sacred, although it happens every day.

Tahirussawichi, Pawnee

Mound Bottom Archaeological Site, Harpeth River State Park, Tennessee

AT THE EDGE OF THE MOUNTAIN
A cloud hangs.
And there my heart, my heart, my heart,
Hangs with it.

At the edge of the mountain
The cloud trembles.
And there my heart, my heart, my heart,
Trembles with it.

Song of the Rain-making Ceremony, Papago

Summit of Mount Langley, Inyo National Forest (Eastern Sierras), California

GOOD NOW! HERE AM I Father (Sun) with my prayer-stick,
We are asking thee for drink.
The glisten of running water is beautiful;
Let the quickening rain, the heavy rain, come.

We have found the water,
All vegetation is beautiful.
The water has entered to the roots,
The Spirit (of the crops) is happy.

The Father (Sun) is watching us;
With his rays comes the water;
The green prayer-stick has brought it.
The corn is beautiful. We are glad.

Song of the Rain-making Ceremony, Hopi

INDIAN VOICES

EVERYTHING THE POWER OF THE World does is done in a circle. The Sky is round and I have heard that the earth is round like a ball and so are all the stars. The Wind, in its greatest power, whirls. Birds make their nests in circles, for theirs is the same religion as ours. The sun comes forth and goes down again in a circle. The moon does the same, and both are round.

Even the seasons form a great circle in their changing, and always come back again to where they were. The life of a man is a circle from childhood to childhood and so it is in everything where power moves. Our tipis were round like the nests of birds and these were always set in a circle, the nation's hoop, a nest of many nests where the Great Spirit meant for us to hatch our children.

Black Elk (Hehaka-sapa), Sioux

FROM THE BEGINNING THERE WERE drums, beating out world rhythm—the booming, never-failing tide on the beach; the four seasons, gliding smoothly, one from the other; when the birds come, when they go, the bear hibernating for his winter sleep. Unfathomable the why, yet all in perfect time.

Watch the heartbeat in your wrist—a precise pulsing beat of life's Drum—with loss of timing you are ill.

Jimalee Burton, Cherokee

THE CIRCLE IS THE SYMBOL OF TIME, for the daytime, the night time, and the moon time are circles above the world, and the year time is a circle around the border of the world.

Sword, Sioux

Cheyenne camp in the
cottonwoods, Tongue River,
Montana, c. 1910

Antelope Canyon, Lake Powell
Navajo Tribal Park, Arizona

INDIAN VOICES

MAY THE SUN RISE WELL
May the earth appear
Brightly shone upon.

May the moon rise well
May the earth appear
Brightly shone upon.

Song of the Sun Dance Ceremony, Sioux

ccc

THE SUNBEAMS STREAM FORWARD, dawn boys,
    with shimmering shoes of yellow.
On top of the sunbeams that stream toward us
    they are dancing.
At the east the rainbow moves forward, dawn maidens,
    with shimmering shoes and shirts of yellow dance over us.
Beautifully over us it is dawning.

Song of the Woman's Puberty Ceremony, Apache

ccc

IT IS ABOVE THAT YOU AND I SHALL GO;
    Along the Milky Way you and I shall go;
It is above that you and I shall go;
    Along the Milky Way you and I shall go.
It is above you and I shall go;
    Along the flower trail you and I shall go.
Picking flowers on our way you and I shall go.

Song of the Dream Dance Ceremony, Wintu

INDIAN VOICES

Look as they rise, rise up
Over the line where sky meets the earth;
Pleiades! Lo! They ascending, come to guide us,
Leading us safely, keeping us one;
Pleiades, Teach us to be, like you, united.

Song of the Calumet Ceremony, Pawnee

We are the stars which sing,
We sing with our light;
We are the birds of fire,
We fly over the sky.
Our light is a voice;
We make a road for spirits,
For the spirits to pass over.
Among us are three hunters
Who chase a bear;
There never was a time
When they were not hunting.
We look down on the mountains.
This is the song of the Stars.

Song of the Stars, Passamaquoddy (Wabanaki)

There were still nights when the Northern Lights swung low across the heavens, and on either side the stars blazed brilliantly in the dark blue sky. . . . On blowy nights the Lights would curl and twist and leap with the wind, and immense ribbons of gold and red would roll and float across the sky. The deeper the winter, the frostier the night, the more brightly glowed the pulsing streamers. . . . To the Eskimos, the Northern Lights proved the existence of a Supreme Power, for they said simply, no man could made the Good Shadows.

Anauta, Inuit (Eskimo)

Northern Lights above Denali National Park and Preserve, Alaska

Grand Canyon National Park,
Arizona

INDIAN VOICES

THAT WIND, THAT WIND
Shakes my tipi, shakes my tipi
And sings a song for me.
And sings a song for me.

Song of the Wind, Kiowa

IT WAS THE WIND THAT GAVE them life. It is the wind that comes out of our mouths now that gives us life. When this ceases to blow we die. In the skin at the tips of our fingers we see the trail of the wind; it shows us where the wind blew when our ancestors were created.

Unidentified Navajo

YOU HEAR THE WIND BLOWING, blowing, then all of a sudden it dies down just as if it had gone off to sleep.

Unidentified Hidatsa

EVERYTHING AS IT MOVES, NOW and then, here and there, makes stops. The bird as it flies stops in one place to make its nest, and in another to rest in its flight. A man when he goes forth stops when he wills. So God has stopped. The sun, which is so bright and beautiful, is one place where he has stopped. The moon, the stars, the winds he has been with. The trees, the animals, are all where he has stopped, and the Indian thinks of these places and send his prayers there to reach the place where God has stopped and to win help and a blessing.

Unidentified Sioux

INDIAN VOICES

Kwakiutl sailing along coast
of British Columbia, c. 1914

THE GREAT SEA
Has sent me adrift.
It moves me as the weed in a great river.
Earth and the great weather
Move me,
Have carried me away
And move my inward parts with joy.

Personal Song of Uvavnuk, Inuit (Eskimo)

BREAKERS, ROLL MORE EASILY.
Don't break so high.
Become quiet.

Song to Calm Rough Seas, Clayoquot

INDIAN VOICES

WHEN I AM OUT OF THE HOUSE in the open,
  I feel joy.
When I get out on the sea on haphazard,
  I feel joy.
If it is really fine weather,
  I feel joy.
If the sky really clears nicely,
  I feel joy.
May it continue thus
  for the good of my sealing!
May it continue thus
  for the good of my hunting!
May it continue thus
  for the good of my singing-match!
May it continue thus
  for the good of my drum-song!

Song to Express Joy, Inuit (Eskimo)

Unknown seal hunter off
Nunivak Island (Eskimo), c. 1929

THESE LAKES, THESE WOODS and mountains, were left to us by our ancestors. They are our inheritance, and we will part with them to none. . . . [H]e—the Great Spirit and master of life—has provided food for us in these broad lakes and upon these mountains.

Minnehwehna, Ojibway

THE GREAT SPIRIT MADE US, the Indians, and gave us this land we live in. He gave us the buffalo, the antelope, and the deer for food and clothing. We moved on our hunting grounds from the Minnesota to the Platte and from the Mississippi to the great mountains. No one put bounds about us. We were free as the winds and like the eagle, heard no man's commands. . . . Where the tipi was, there we stayed and no house imprisoned us. No one said, "To this line is my land, to that is yours." In this way our fathers lived and were happy.

Red Cloud, Sioux

INDIAN VOICES

Fighting antelope (pronghorn)

Buffalo (bison)

INDIAN VOICES

TATANKA, THE BUFFALO, IS THE CLOSEST four-legged relative we have, and they live as a people, as we do. The buffalo represents the people and the universe and should always be treated with respect, for was he not here before the two-legged peoples, and is he not generous in that he gives us our homes and food? The buffalo is wise in many things, and, thus, we should learn from him and should always be as a relative with him.

Black Elk (Hehaka-sapa), Sioux

WE LAKOTA HAVE A CLOSE RELATIONSHIP to the buffalo. He is our brother. You can't understand about nature, about the feeling we have toward it, unless you understand how close we were to the buffalo. That animal was almost like a part of ourselves, part of our souls.

Lame Deer, Sioux

LOOK YOU, MY GRANDFATHERS RISE,
They of the shaggy manes, rise quickly;
Look you, my grandfathers rise,
They of the curved horns, rise quickly;

Look you, my grandfathers rise,
They of the humped shoulders, rise quickly;
Look you, my grandfathers rise,
They whose tails curl in anger, rise quickly;

Look you, my grandfathers rise,
They, the four-legged ones, rise quickly;
Look you, my grandfathers rise,
They who paw the earth in anger, rise quickly.

Song of the Buffalo Bull Clan, Osage

INDIAN VOICES

THE BUFFALO LIKED TO WALLOW their big heads in the sunflowers, and many times saw them with long stems wound about the left horn, for they never wore them on the right horn. Perhaps they did this to decorate themselves, or maybe they liked the smell of the flowers. We only knew that they liked the sunflower.

Luther Standing Bear, Sioux

C C C

WHEN I WAS SOMEWHAT PAST TEN years of age, my father took me with him to watch the horses out on the prairie. We watered the herd and about the middle of the day came home for dinner. . . . While we sat watching the herd my father said: "These horses are godlike, or mystery beings."

Wolf Chief, Hidatsa

Wild horses (mustangs)

INDIAN VOICES

Riders on Cheyenne Reservation, Montana, c. 1910

TO BE ALONE WITH OUR WAR-HORSES . . . them to understand us, and us to understand them. . . . [I]f he is to carry me in battle he must know my heart and I must know his or we shall never become brothers. I have been told that the white man, who is almost a god, and yet a great fool, does not believe that the horse has a spirit. This cannot be true. I have many times seen my horse's soul in his eyes.

Plenty Coups, Crow

ccc

MY FATHER EXPLAINED THIS TO ME. "All things in this world," he said, "have souls or spirits. The sky has a spirit; the clouds have spirits; the sun and moon have spirits; so have animals, trees, grass, water, stones, everything."

Edward Goodbird, Hidatsa

Unknown Sioux, near Badlands,
South Dakota, c. 1905

INDIAN VOICES

FRIEND
My horse
Flies like a bird
As it runs.

Song of the Horse Society, Sioux

ϲϲϲ

SEE THEM
Prancing, they come
Neighing, they come
A Horse nation
See them
Prancing, they come
Neighing, they come.

Song of the Horse Society, Sioux

ϲϲϲ

OF ALL THE ANIMALS THE HORSE is the best friend
of the Indian, for without it he could not go
on long journeys. A horse is the Indian's most
valuable piece of property. If an Indian wishes to
gain something, he promises his horse that if the
horse will help him he will paint it with native
dye, that all may see that help has come to him
through the aid of his horse.

Brave Buffalo (Tatanka-ohitika), Sioux

THE CROW COUNTRY IS A GOOD country. The Great
Spirit has put it exactly in the right place. . . . When the
summer heats scorch the prairies, you can draw up under
the mountains, where the air is sweet and cool, the grass
fresh, and the bright streams come tumbling out of the
snow banks. There you can hunt the elk, the deer, and the
antelope. . . . In the autumn, when your horses are fat and
strong from the mountain pastures, you can go down
into the plains and hunt buffalo, or trap beaver on the
streams. And when winter comes on, you can take shelter
in the woody bottoms along the rivers; there you will find
buffalo meat for yourselves, and cottonwood bark for your
horses. . . . The Crow Country is exactly in the right place.
Everything good is to be found there.

Arapooish, Crow

OUR FATHER, CREATOR SUN, is the only Creator of all life, one maker. . . . There is no one like our Creator Sun. He alone gave us a commandment that was to be used by all, especially the human beings. The commandment was just a plain "Be honest to life and to all life." This one commandment covered everything: be honest.

Percy Bullchild, Blackfoot

MY FATHER? THE SUN IS MY father, the earth is my mother, and on her bosom I will recline.

Tecumseh, Shawnee

Buffalo berry gatherers
(Mandan) on Fort Berthold
Reservation, North Dakota, 1908

INDIAN VOICES

GOD CREATED THE INDIAN COUNTRY and it was like He spread out a big blanket. He put the Indians on it. . . . Then God created fish in this river and put deer in the mountains and made laws through which has come the increase of fish and game. Then the Creator gave us Indians life; we walked, and as soon as we saw the game and fish we knew they were made for us. For the women God made roots and berries to gather, and the Indians grew and multiplied as a people. . . .

My mother gathered berries; my father fished and killed the game. These words are mine and they are true. . . . My strength is from the fish; my blood is from the fish, from the roots and the berries. The fish and game are the essence of my life. . . . Whenever the seasons open I raise my heart in thanks to the Creator of His bounty that this food has come.

George Meninock, Yakama

IRON BULL, A LITTLE BOY MY AGE, and I had great fun fishing. We always made an offering of bait to the fish, saying: "You who are down in the water with wings of red, I offer this to you; so come hither." Then when we caught the first fish, we would put it on a forked stick and kiss it. If we did not do this, we were sure the others would know and stay away. If we caught a little fish, we would kiss it and throw it back, so that it would not go and frighten the bigger fish. I don't know whether all this helped or not, but we always got plenty of fish, and our parents were proud of us.

Black Elk (Hehaka-sapa), Sioux

Chisos Mountains, Big Bend
National Park, Texas

I WAS BORN ON THE PRAIRIE where the wind blew free and
there was nothing to break the light of the sun. I was born
where there were no enclosures and where everything drew
a free breath. I want to die there and not within walls. I know
every stream and every wood between the Rio Grande and
the Arkansas. I have hunted and lived over the country. I lived
like my fathers before me, and like them, I lived happily.

Ten Bears (Paruasemena), Comanche

FROM MY BOYHOOD I HAVE OBSERVED leaves, trees, and grass, and I have never found two alike. They may have a general likeness, but on examination I have found that they differ slightly. Plants are of different families, each being adapted to growth in a certain locality. It is the same with animals . . . [and] with human beings; there is some place which is best adapted to each. The seeds of the plants are blown about by the wind until they reach the place where they will grow best—where the action of the sun and the presence of moisture are most favorable to them, and there they take root and grow.

Shooter, Sioux

INDIAN VOICES

I AM AN OLD WOMAN NOW. The buffaloes and black-tail deer are gone, and our Indian ways are almost gone. Sometimes I find it hard to believe that I ever lived them. . . . Often in summer I rise at daybreak and steal out to the corn fields, and as I hoe the corn I sing to it, as we did when I was young. . . . Sometimes in the evening I sit, looking out on the big Missouri. The sun sets, and dusk steals over the water. In the shadows I seem again to see our Indian village, with smoke curling upward from the earth lodges, and in the river's roar I hear the yells of the warriors, and the laughter of little children as of old. It is but an old woman's dream.

Buffalo Bird (Waheenee), Hidatsa

Pawnee earth lodges on the Loup Fork
of the Platte River, Nebraska, 1871

INDIAN VOICES

WE WHO ARE CLAY BLENDED BY THE Master Potter come from the kiln of Creation in many hues. How can people say one skin is colored, when each has its own coloration? What should it matter that one bowl is dark and the other pale, if each is of good design and serves its purpose well?

Polingaysi Qoyawayma (Elizabeth White), Hopi

INDIAN VOICES

THE GREAT MYSTERY IS EVERYWHERE. He is in the earth and the water, heat and cold, rocks and trees, sun and sky; and he is also in us. There are wonders all about us, and within, but if we are quiet and obedient to the voice of the spirit, sometimes we may understand these mysteries!

Ohiyesa (Charles Eastman), Sioux

THERE ARE BIRDS OF MANY COLORS—red, blue, green, yellow—yet it is all one bird. There are horses of many colors—brown, black, yellow, white—yet it is all one horse. So cattle, so all living things—animals, flowers, trees. So men: in this land where once were only Indians are now men of every color—white, black, yellow, red—yet all one people. That this should come to pass was in the heart of the Great Mystery. It is right thus. And everywhere there shall be peace.

High Chief (Hiamovi), Cheyenne

Northern pintail duck

INDIAN VOICES

ALL BIRDS, EVEN THOSE of the same species, are not alike, and it is the same with animals and with human beings. The reason Wakan Tanka does not make two birds, or animals, or human beings exactly alike is because each is placed here by Wakan Tanka to be an independent individuality and to rely upon itself.

Shooter, Sioux

THE MOST IMPORTANT OF ALL THE creatures are the wingeds, for they are nearest to the heavens, and are not bound to the earth as are the four-leggeds, or the little crawling people. It may be good to mention here that it is not without reason that we humans are two-legged along with the wingeds; for you see the birds leave the earth with their wings, and we humans may also leave this world, not with wings, but in the spirit.

Black Elk (Hehaka-sapa), Sioux

White-crowned sparrow

Mature bald eagle

INDIAN VOICES

WHEN THE SEASON RETURNS, the birds and insects return with the same colorings as the previous year. They are not all on the earth, but are above it. My mind must be the same.

Siyaka, Sioux

[THE EAGLE] SPREADS HIS WINGS and soars aloft and breathes deep with the joy of well-being. The eagle is myself. God has given me that bird. I have taken the eagle for my bird because he is the greatest of all birds. He is the father, and all little birds are his children. He is strong, for he flies where no man can reach him. He is clean, for he spreads his wings when he eats that no dirt may fall upon his food, and he washes his claws in the mud of streams. In his feathers, white and black, we see day and night. That is why I carry the fan of eagle feathers.

Magpie (Mowihaiz), Cheyenne

BIRDS, I LOVE TO SEE THE BIRDS, because they are pretty. They do not say anything evil. They eat these things Mundu gives, then they sing, because they do not want for anything. All things Mundu gives them, that is so. All things!

Flying Bird (Fidelia Fielding), Mohegan

THE LARK IS CHEERFUL AND BRINGS the warm weather. It does not scold its people. It is always happy.

Unidentified Sioux

INDIAN VOICES

[T]HE VOICE OF THE GREAT SPIRIT IS heard in the twittering of birds, the rippling of mighty waters, and the sweet breathing of flowers. If this is Paganism, then at present, at least, I am a Pagan.

Zitkala-sa (Gertrude Bonnin), Sioux

[T]HE YELLOWHAMMER CANNOT overcome its enemies in open flight but is expert at dodging them, darting from one side of the tree-trunk to another.

Lone Man, Sioux

NOW, SOME PEOPLE MAY THINK that human beings were the first to dance, but I do not think so. I believe that the birds danced first. . . . I have seen the prairie chickens hold dances as orderly and as well organized as I have seen humans hold.

Luther Standing Bear, Sioux

WAKAN TANKA TEACHES THE BIRDS to make nests, yet the nests of all birds are not alike. Wakan Tanka gives them merely the outline. Some birds make better nests than others.

Shooter, Sioux

Great blue heron

Cliff Palace, Mesa Verde
National Park, Colorado

INDIAN VOICES

THE AMERICAN INDIAN IS OF THE SOIL, whether it be the region of forests, plains, pueblos, or mesas. He fits into the landscape, for the hand that fashioned the continent also fashioned the man for his surroundings. He once grew as naturally as the wild sunflowers; he belongs just as the buffalo belonged.

Luther Standing Bear, Sioux

ccc

FAIR AS IS THE CLEAR SKY, the green grass, yet more fair is peace among men.

Song of the Calumet Ceremony, Omaha

ccc

BEHOLD, MY BROTHERS, the spring has come; the earth has received the embraces of the sun and we shall soon see the results of that love!

Every seed is awakened and so has all animal life. It is through this mysterious power that we too have our being and we therefore yield to our neighbors, even our animal neighbors, the same right as ourselves, to inhabit this land.

Sitting Bull, Sioux

INDIAN VOICES

My words are tied in one
With the great mountains,
With the great rocks,
With the great trees,
In one with my body
And my heart.
Do you all help me
With supernatural power
And you, day,
And you, night,
All of you see me
One with this world!

Unidentified Yokuts

The rock did not come here by itself.
The tree does not stand here of itself.
There is one who made all of this,
Who shows us everything.

Song of the Obsidian Ceremony, Yuki

All things declare Mundu has made them. I can
not make myself, they declare man can not make
one tree. I see another sun because Mundu is good
exceedingly. Man does not make but little. He thinks
he knows much. That is so.

Flying Bird (Fidelia Fielding), Mohegan

Summit of Gray Peak,
Adirondack Park, New York

Unknown Crow overlooking Black
Canyon, Wyoming, c. 1905

INDIAN VOICES

WHEN I WAS TEN YEARS of age I looked at the land and the rivers, the sky above, and the animals around me and could not fail to realize that they were made by some great power. I was so anxious to understand this power that I questioned the trees and the bushes. It seemed as though the flowers were staring at me, and I wanted to ask them "Who made you?" I looked at the moss-covered stones; some of them seemed to have the features of a man, but they could not answer me. Then I had a dream, and in my dream one of these small round stones appeared to me and told me that the maker of all was Wakan Tanka, and that in order to honor him I must honor his works in nature.

Brave Buffalo (Tatanka-ohitika), Sioux

WE BELIEVED IN A POWER that was higher than all people and all the created world, and we called this power the Man-Above. We believed in some power in the world that governed everything that grew, and we called this power Mother-Earth. We believed in the power of the Sun, of the Night-Sun or Moon, of the Morning Star, and of the Four Old Men who direct the winds and the rains and the seasons and give us the breath of life. We believed that everything created is holy and has some part in the power that is over all.

Carl Sweezy, Arapaho

INDIAN VOICES

THE GREAT SPIRIT FIRST MADE the world, and
next the flying animals, and found all things
good and prosperous. He is immortal and
everlasting. After finishing the flying animals,
he came down on earth and there stood. Then
he made different kinds of trees, and weeds
of all sorts, and people of every kind. He made
the spring and other seasons, and the weather
suitable for planting. . . .

When the Great Spirit had made the earth
and its animals, he went into the great lakes,
where he breathed as easily as anywhere else,
and then made all the different kinds of fish. . . .
He is the cause of all things that exist, and it is
very wicked to go against His will.

Cornplanter, Seneca (Iroquois)

As A NEZ PERCE MAN PASSED through the
forest the moving trees whispered to him and
his heart swelled with the song of the swaying
pine. He looked through the green branches
and saw white clouds drifting across the blue
dome, and he felt the song of the clouds. Each
bird twittering in the branches, each water-fowl
among the reeds or on the surface of the lake,
spoke its intelligible message to his heart; and
as he looked into the sky and saw the high-
flying birds of passage, he knew that their flight
was made strong by the uplifted voices of ten
thousand birds of the meadow, forest, and
lake, and his heart, fairly in tune with all this,
vibrated with the songs of its fullness.

Chief Joseph (Rolling Thunder), Nez Perce

INDIAN VOICES

Tahquamenon Falls State Park, Michigan

INDIAN VOICES

We BELIEVED THAT THE SPIRIT pervades all creation and that every creature possesses a soul in some degree, though not necessarily a soul conscious of itself. The tree, the waterfall, the grizzly bear, each is an embodied Force, and as such an object of reverence.

Ohiyesa (Charles Eastman), Sioux

The LAKOTA COULD DESPISE NO creature, for all were of one blood, made by the same hand, and filled with the essence of the Great Mystery.

Luther Standing Bear, Sioux

Black bear

Bear's Belly,
Arikara, c. 1908

THE GREAT SPIRIT IS IN ALL THINGS; he is in the air we breathe. The Great Spirit is our Father, but the earth is our mother. She nourishes us; that which we put into the ground she returns to us, and healing plants she gives us likewise. If we are wounded, we go to our mother and seek to lay the wounded part against her, to be healed.

Big Thunder (Bedagi), Penobscot (Wabanaki)

INDIAN VOICES

WE DO NOT WALK ALONE. Great Being walks beside us. Know this and be grateful.

Polingaysi Qoyawayma (Elizabeth White), Hopi

ccc

ALL LIVING CREATURES AND ALL plants derive their life from the sun. If it were not for the sun, there would be darkness and nothing could grow—the earth would be without life. Yet the sun must have the help of the earth. If the sun alone were to act upon animals and plants, the heat would be so great that they would die, but there are clouds that bring rain, and the action of the sun and earth together supply the moisture that is needed for life. The roots of a plant go down, and the deeper they go the more moisture they find. This is according to the laws of nature and is one of the evidences of the wisdom of Wakan Tanka. Plants are sent by Wakan Tanka and come from the ground at his command, the part to be affected by the sun and rain appearing above the ground and the roots pressing downward to find the moisture which is supplied for them. Animals and plants are taught by Wakan Tanka what they are to do.

Shooter, Sioux

ccc

WITH THE INDIAN WAY, YOU don't have to go to church in order to pray. You can step outside, anytime. . . . I can sit under my pine trees here and offer my prayers, and my prayers are answered. I don't have to go into a church or cathedral just on Sunday. I can go out two or three times a day. If something bothers me, I can go out there and pray and I'm sure I'm being heard. It's a portable church. As far as I'm concerned, there is no better church here on this place except under these pine trees.

Susie (Walking Bear) Yellowtail, Crow

Hell Hollow Wilderness
Area, Ohio

INDIAN VOICES

McWay Falls in Julia Pfeiffer Burns
State Park (Big Sur), California

INDIAN VOICES

WE THANK THE GREAT SPIRIT for all the benefits He confers upon us. For myself, I never take a drink of water from a spring, without being mindful of His goodness.

Black Hawk, Sauk

WHILE LIVING I WANT TO LIVE well. I know I have to die some time, but even if the heavens were to fall on me, I want to do what is right. . . . There is one God looking down on us all. We are children of the one God. God is listening to me. The sun, the darkness, the winds are all listening to what we now say.

Geronimo, Apache

WHEN A MAN DOES A PIECE of work which is admired by all we say that it is wonderful; but when we see the changes of day and night, the sun, moon, and stars in the sky, and the changing seasons upon the earth, with their ripening fruits, anyone must realize that it is the work of some one more powerful than man.

Chased-by-Bears, Sioux

INDIAN VOICES

CIVILIZED PEOPLE DEPEND TOO much on man-made printed pages. I turn to the Great Spirit's book, which is the whole of His creation. You can read a big part of that book if you study nature. You know, if you take all your books, lay them out under the sun, and let the snow and rain and insects work on them for a while, there will be nothing left. But the Great Spirit has provided you and me with an opportunity for study in nature's university, the forests, the rivers, the mountains, and the animals, which include us.

Walking Buffalo (Tatanka-mani), Stoney

A MAN'S ATTITUDE TOWARD the nature around him, and the animals in nature, is of special importance, because as we respect our created world, so also do we show respect for the real world that we cannot see.

Thomas Yellowtail, Crow

FROM WAKAN TANKA, THE Great Mystery, comes all power. It is from Wakan Tanka that the Holy Man has wisdom and the power to heal and to make holy charms. Man knows that all healing plants are given by Wakan Tanka; therefore are they holy. So too is the buffalo holy, because it is the gift of Wakan Tanka. The Great Mystery gave to men all things for their food, their clothing, and their welfare. And to man he gave also the knowledge how to use these gifts—how to find the holy healing plants, how to hunt and surround the buffalo, how to know wisdom. For all comes from Wakan Tanka—all.

Flat Iron (Maza-blaska), Sioux

Unknown Mandan on Fort Berthold
Reservation, North Dakota, c. 1908

INDIAN VOICES

Sun Dance lodge, Crow
Reservation, Montana, c. 1960

WE SHOULD UNDERSTAND WELL that all things are the works
of the Great Spirit. We should know that He is within all
things: the trees, the grasses, the rivers, the mountains, and all
the four-legged animals, and the winged peoples; and even
more important, we should understand that He is also above
all these things and peoples.

Black Elk (Hehaka-sapa), Sioux

INDIAN VOICES

BROTHER, LISTEN TO WHAT WE SAY. There was a time when our forefathers owned this great island. Their seats extended from the rising to the setting sun. The Great Spirit had made it for the use of Indians. He had created the buffalo, the deer, and other animals for food. He had made the bear and beaver. Their skins served us for clothing. He had scattered them over the country and taught us how to take them. He had caused the earth to produce corn for bread. All this He had done for His red children because He loved them.

Red Jacket (Sagoyewatha), Seneca (Iroquois)

Mikasuki (Seminole) village, Big
Cypress Swamp, Florida, c. 1920

INDIAN VOICES

WHENEVER, IN THE COURSE OF the daily hunt the red hunter comes upon a scene that is strikingly beautiful or sublime—a black thundercloud with the rainbow's glowing arch above the mountain, a white waterfall in the heart of a green gorge, a vast prairie tinged with the blood-red of sunset—he pauses for an instant in the attitude of worship. He sees no need for setting apart one day in seven as a holy day, since to him all days are God's.

Ohiyesa (Charles Eastman), Sioux

BEFORE PROCEEDING IN THE HUNT, it was necessary to stop, take a smoke, and offer a prayer to the Medicine Fathers. They will always hear the prayer of a sincere hunter and help the hunter to find success. It is not through the great skill of the hunter himself that success is achieved, but through the hunter's awareness of his place in Creation and his relationship to all things.

Thomas Yellowtail, Crow

Bear Lodge, Wyoming

Bobcat (lynx)

WHEN THE HUNTER GOES into the woods to hunt . . . and he sees a black bear he shoots it. As soon as he has killed it, then the hunter goes to where the bear that he has shot lies dead and stands by its side and says, "Thank you, friend, that we met. I did not mean to do you any harm, friend. Indeed, this is the reason why you come, made by our creator, that I may come to shoot you, that I may eat you, with my wife, friend."

Unidentified Kwakiutl

OH FRIENDS! THANK YOU that we meet alive. We have lived until this time when you came this year. . . . For that is the reason why you come here, that we may catch you for food. We know that only your bodies are dead here, but your souls come to watch over us when we are going to eat what you have given us to eat now.

Unidentified Kwakiutl

Unknown Qahatika (Pima)
gathering hasen in Sonoran
Desert, Arizona, c. 1907

INDIAN VOICES

THERE IS A REASON TO HUNT, but if you just want to kill for fun, you should not hunt. We were given animals for a purpose, and through our knowledge of animals and nature, we come closer to the Maker of All Things Above.

Thomas Yellowtail, Crow

WE RETURN THANKS TO THE Three Sisters. We thank thee that thou hast provided them as the main supporters of our lives. We thank thee for the abundant harvest gathered in during the past season. We ask that Our Supporters may never fail us, and cause our children to suffer from want.

Sosehawa, Seneca (Iroquois)

EVEN BEFORE YOU PLANT YOU sing songs. You continue this during the whole time your crops are growing. You cannot help but feel that you are in a holy place when you go through your fields and they are doing well.

Peter Prince, Navajo

THE BEAR IS QUICK-TEMPERED and is fierce in many ways, and yet he pays attention to herbs which no other animal notices at all. . . . The bear is the only animal which eats roots from the earth and is also especially fond of acorns, june berries, and cherries. These three are frequently compounded with other herbs in making medicine, and if a person is fond of cherries we say he is like a bear. We consider the bear as chief of all animals in regard to herb medicine, and therefore it is understood that if a man dreams of a bear he will be expert in the use of herbs for curing illness.

Siyaka, Sioux

INDIAN VOICES

AT ONE TIME ANIMALS AND men were able to understand each other. We can still talk to the animals just as we do to people, but they now seldom reply, excepting in dreams. . . . Whenever we are in danger, or distress, we pray to them and they often help us.

Brings-down-the-Sun, Blackfoot

MAN LIVES ON THE FRUITS of the earth; this is true when he feeds on the animals, for all draw their nourishment from mother earth; our bodies are strengthened by animal food and our powers can be strengthened by the animals giving us of their peculiar gifts, for each animal has received from Wakonda some special gift. If a man asks help of Wakonda, Wakonda will send the asker the animal that has the gift that will help the man in his need.

Unidentified Omaha

SOMETIMES MEN SAY THAT they can understand the meaning of the songs of birds. I can believe this is true. They say that they can understand the call and cry of the animals, and I can believe this also is true, for these creatures and man are alike the work of a great power.

Chased-by-Bears, Sioux

Petroglyphs in
Newspaper Rock
State Historic
Monument, Utah

Florida panther (puma)

I HAVE NOTICED IN MY LIFE that all men have a liking for some special animal, tree, plant, or spot of earth. If men would pay more attention to these preferences and seek what is best to do in order to make themselves worthy of that toward which they are so attracted, they might have dreams which would purify their lives. Let a man decide upon his favorite animal and make a study of it, learning its innocent ways. Let him learn to understand its sounds and motions. The animals want to communicate with man, but Wakan Tanka does not intend they shall do so directly—man must do the greater part in securing an understanding.

Brave Buffalo (Tatanka-ohitika), Sioux

YOU HAVE TO LISTEN TO ALL these creatures, listen with your mind. They have secrets to tell.

Lame Deer, Sioux

INDIAN VOICES

IN HIS NATIVE STATE THE ELK has a very proud and independent manner. He walks about among his herd as if there is nothing in the sky nor on earth that is his equal. And others of the herd seem to think so too. Even when feeding, he never seems to forget his dignity. With every mouthful of food, up goes his head as he watches over his herd.

Luther Standing Bear, Sioux

THE ELK IS THE EMBLEM OF beauty, gallantry, and protection. The elk lives in the forest and is in harmony with all his beautiful surroundings. He goes easily through the thickets, notwithstanding his broad branching horns.

Shooter, Sioux

THE BULL ELK IS BRAVE, ALWAYS helping his women, and in this way he has saved a large number of his people. In this I should follow the bull elk, remembering that he is my helper.

Siyaka, Sioux

INDIAN VOICES

Bull elk bugling

INDIAN VOICES

[A]LL ANIMALS HAVE POWER, because the Great Spirit dwells in all of them, even a tiny ant, a butterfly, a tree, a flower, a rock. . . . To come to nature, feel its power, let it help you, one needs time and patience for that.

Pete Catches, Sioux

ccc

ONE SHOULD PAY ATTENTION to even the smallest crawling creature for these may have a valuable lesson to teach us, and even the smallest ant may wish to communicate to a man.

Black Elk (Hehaka-sapa), Sioux

Red squirrel

INDIAN VOICES

Spider web in morning dew

THE SPIDER IS INDUSTRIOUS and builds a tipi for its children. It provides them with plenty of food.

Unidentified Sioux

San Joaquin kit fox

INDIAN VOICES

THE TURTLE IS WISE AND HEARS many things and does not tell anything. Its skin is like a shield so that arrows cannot wound it.

Unidentified Sioux

THE FOX HAD KNOWLEDGE OF underground things hidden from human eyes, and this he shared with the dreamer, telling him of roots and herbs that are good in healing; then he shared his powers of swiftness and cleverness as well as gentleness.

Luther Standing Bear, Sioux

[Y]OU OUGHT TO FOLLOW THE EXAMPLE of the *shunktokecha* (wolf). Even when he is surprised and runs for his life, he will pause to take one more look at you before he enters his final retreat. So you must take a second look at everything you see.

Ohiyesa (Charles Eastman), Sioux

IN A DREAM VOICES TOLD ME that the frog must not be harmed, as he watches everything in the water and has been given this peculiar power. They also told me a great deal about the creatures that live in the water, saying they are taken care of, and water is sent them from the sky when they need it; therefore they should never be treated cruelly.

Lone Man, Sioux

INDIAN VOICES

[T]HE RABBIT REPRESENTS HUMILITY, because he is quiet and soft and not self-asserting—a quality which we must all possess.

Black Elk (Hehaka-sapa), Sioux

THE ANIMALS HAD RIGHTS: THE right of man's protection, the right to live, the right to multiply, the right to freedom, the right to man's gratitude. In recognition of these rights people never enslaved the animals, and spared all life that was not needed for food and clothing.

Luther Standing Bear, Sioux

DO NOT HARM YOUR WEAKER brothers, for even a little squirrel may be the bearer of good fortune!

Ohiyesa (Charles Eastman), Sioux

ALL LIVING CREATURES AND all plants are a benefit to something.

Shooter, Sioux

INDIAN VOICES

White-tailed deer fawn

Unknown Seminole canoeing on
Miami River, Florida, c. 1904

INDIAN VOICES

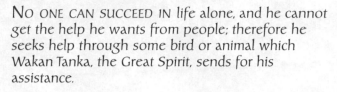

NO ONE CAN SUCCEED IN life alone, and he cannot get the help he wants from people; therefore he seeks help through some bird or animal which Wakan Tanka, the Great Spirit, sends for his assistance.

Siyaka, Sioux

IN THE BEGINNING OF ALL THINGS, wisdom and knowledge were with the animals, for Tirawa, the One Above, did not speak directly to man. He sent certain animals to tell men that he showed himself through the beasts, and that from them, and from the stars and the sun and the moon should man learn. Tirawa spoke to man through his works, and the Pawnee understands the heavens, the beasts, and the plants. For all things tell of Tirawa.

Eagle Chief (Letakots-lesa), Pawnee

THERE IS NOT A LAKE OR MOUNTAIN that has not connected with it some story of delight and wonder, and nearly every beast and bird is the subject of the story-teller.

George Copway (Kahgegagahbowh), Ojibwa

Bryce Canyon National Park, Utah

We know our lands have now become more valuable. The white people think we do not know their value; but we are sensible that the land is everything, and the few goods we receive for it are soon worn out and gone. For the future we will sell no lands.

Canassatego, Onondaga (Iroquois)

SELL A COUNTRY! WHY NOT sell the air, the clouds and the great sea, as well as the earth? Did not the Great Spirit make them all for the use of his children?

Tecumseh, Shawnee

INDIAN VOICES

Burial platform, Crow Reservation,
Montana, c. 1908

I NEVER WANT TO LEAVE THIS COUNTRY; all my relatives are
lying here in the ground, and when I fall to pieces I am going
to fall to pieces here.

Wolf Necklace (Shunkaha-napin), Sioux

THE GROUND ON WHICH WE STAND is sacred ground. It is the
dust and blood of our ancestors. . . . A few more passing suns
will see us here no more, and our dust and bones will mingle
with these same prairies.

Plenty Coups, Crow

INDIAN VOICES

THE SOIL YOU SEE IS NOT ORDINARY soil; it is the dust of the blood, the flesh, and bones of our ancestors. . . . You will have to dig down through the surface before you can find nature's earth, as the upper portion is Crow. The land, as it is, is my blood and my dead; it is consecrated.

Curley, Crow

MY FRIENDS, ONLY THE STONES stay on earth forever. Use your best ability.

Song of the Warrior, Cheyenne

Pre-historic serpent effigy mound, Ohio

INDIAN VOICES

I WAS BORN IN *NATURE'S WIDE domain!* The trees were all that sheltered my infant limbs—the blue heavens all that covered me. I am one of Nature's children; I have always admired her; she shall be my glory; her features—her robes, and the wreath about her brow— the seasons—her stately oaks, and the evergreen—her hair—ringlets over the earth—all contribute to my enduring love of her; and wherever I see her, emotions of pleasure roll in my breast, and swell and burst like waves on the shores of the ocean, in prayer and praise to Him, who has placed me in her hand. . . .

I would much more glory in this birthplace, with the broad canopy of heaven above me, and the giant arms of the forest trees for my shelter, than to be born in palaces of marble, studded with pillars of gold! Nature will be Nature still, while palaces shall decay and fall in ruins.

Yes, Niagara will be Niagara a thousand years hence! The rainbow, a wreath over her brow, shall continue as long as the sun, and the flowing of the river! While the work of art, however impregnable, shall fade and crumble into dust!

George Copway (Kahgegagahbowh), Ojibwa

INDIAN VOICES

Niagara Falls, Ontario/New York

INDIAN VOICES

Black Hills National Forest,
South Dakota

INDIAN VOICES

ALL MEN WERE MADE BY THE same Great Spirit Chief. They are all brothers. The earth is the mother of all people, and all people should have equal rights upon it. You might as well expect the rivers to run backwards as that any man who was born a free man should be contented when penned up and denied liberty to go where he pleases.

Chief Joseph (Rolling Thunder), Nez Perce

I DON'T WANT TO SETTLE. I LOVE to roam over the prairies. There I feel free and happy, but when we settle down we grow pale and die.

White Bear (Santanta), Kiowa

Sioux camp near Wounded Knee,
South Dakota, 1891

CONTEMPORARY VOICES

EVERY NATION HAS A SPIRIT. The Mohegan spirit moves and breathes within the rocks and trees of the Mohegan homeland. That sacred landscape has been crushed and trampled for four centuries by non-Indian invaders who have denied the inherent spiritual value of that plot of earth. To Mohegans, land is the fabric upon which the designs of religious beliefs and patterns of history are colorfully woven.

Melissa Tantaquidgeon Zobel, Mohegan Medicine Woman and Tribal Historian

CCC

I SPENT MY LIFE RESPECTING the earth, protecting it, and at times living off the land. My most introspective moments, indeed my most vulnerable moments, have been when I was alone with my thoughts in the woods—sometimes cold and hungry—but the earth and the sun made sure I was never alone, that I was fed, watered, and warmed, and nature always kept me strong. As a twenty-first century Native American, I am as respectful of Mother Earth as those from our past whose very existence depended daily on everything the earth provided . . . and am reminded as we look to Standing Rock that even in the present, as we tend to forget that dependence, it still exists.

Red Eagle (Kevin Brown), Mohegan Tribal Chairman

SPEAKERS

TRIBES

PLACES

PHOTOGRAPHERS

SOURCES

Assikinack, Francis. "Social and Warlike Customs of the Odahwah Indians". *The Canadian Journal of Industry, Science, and Art*, Vol. 3. Toronto: The Canadian Institute, 1858.

Ayer, I. Winslow. *Life in the Wilds of America: And Wonders of the West in and Beyond the Bounds of Civilization*. Grand Rapids: Central Publishing, 1880.

Bass, Althea. *The Arapaho Way: A Memoir of an Indian Boyhood*. New York: Clarkson N. Potter, 1966.

Boas, Franz. *Ethnology of the Kwakiutl*. Smithsonian Institution, Bureau of American Ethnology, Thirty-fifth Annual Report, Pts. 1 and 2. Washington: U.S. Government Printing Office, 1921.

———. *The Religion of the Kwakiutl Indians*. New York: Columbia University Press, 1930.

Boyd, Julian P. (ed.). *Indian Treaties Printed by Benjamin Franklin, 1736-1762*. Philadelphia: Historical Society of Pennsylvania, 1938.

Brown, Joseph E. (ed.). *The Sacred Pipe: Black Elk's Account of the Seven Rites of the Oglala Sioux*. Norman: University of Oklahoma Press, 1953.

Bullchild, Percy. *The Sun Came Down: The History of the World as My Blackfeet Elders Told It*. San Francisco: Harper & Row, 1985.

Burlin, Natalie C. (ed.). *The Indians' Book: An Offering by the American Indians of Indian Lore, Musical and Narrative*. New York: Harper and Brothers Publishers, 1907.

Burton, Jimalee. *Indian Heritage, Indian Pride: Stories That Touched My Life*. Norman, OK: The University of Oklahoma Press, 1974.

Copway, George. *The Life, History, and Travels of Kah-ge-ga-gah-bowh (George Copway)*. Albany: Weed and Parsons, 1847.

———. *The Traditional History and Characteristic Sketches of the Ojibway Nation*. Boston: Benjamin B. Mussey, 1851.

Curtis, Edward S. *The North American Indian: Being a Series of Volumes Picturing and Describing the Indians of the United States and Alaska*, Vol. 8. Norwood, MA: 1911.

Demetracopoulou, Dorothy. "Wintu Songs". *Anthropos*, Vol. 30, 1935.

Densmore, Francis. *Nootka and Quileute Music.* Smithsonian Institution, Bureau of American Ethnology, Bulletin 124. Washington: U.S. Government Printing Office, 1939.

———. *Music of Acoma, Isleta, Cochiti and Zuni Pueblos.* Smithsonian Institution, Bureau of American Ethnology, Bulletin 165. Washington: U.S. Government Printing Office, 1957.

———. *Teton Sioux Music.* Smithsonian Institution, Bureau of American Ethnology, Bulletin 61. Washington: U.S. Government Printing Office, 1918.

Dixon, Joseph K. *The Vanishing Race: The Last Great Indian Council.* Garden City, NY: Doubleday, Page, 1913.

Eastman, Charles A. *Indian Boyhood.* New York: McClure, Phillips, 1902.

———. *The Soul of the Indian: An Interpretation.* Boston: Houghton Mifflin, 1911.

———. & Eastman, Elaine Goodale. *Wigwam Evenings: Sioux Tales Retold.* Boston: Little, Brown, 1909.

Fitzgerald, Michael O. (ed.). *Yellowtail: Crow Medicine Man and Sun Dance Chief, An Autobiography.* Norman: University of Oklahoma Press, 1991.

Fletcher, Alice C. "The Elk Mystery or Festival of the Ogallala Sioux". Peabody Museum of American Archaeology and Ethnology, Seventeenth and Eighteenth Annual Reports, Vol. 3, Nos. 3 & 4. Cambridge: 1884.

———. *The Hako: A Pawnee Ceremony.* Smithsonian Institution, Bureau of American Ethnology, Twenty-second Annual Report, Pt. 2. Washington: U.S. Government Printing Office, 1904.

———. & La Flesche, Francis. *The Omaha Tribe.* Smithsonian Institution, Bureau of American Ethnology, Twenty-seventh Annual Report. Washington: U.S. Government Printing Office, 1911.

Ganter, Granville (ed.). *The Collected Speeches of Sagoyewatha, Or Red Jacket.* Syracuse: Syracuse University Press, 2006.

Goddard, Pliny. *Gotal: A Mescalero Apache Ceremony.* Cedar Rapids: The Torch Press, 1909.

Goodbird, Edward. *Goodbird the Indian: His Story*, ed. Gilbert L. Wilson. New York: Fleming H. Revel, 1914.

Gostwick, Joseph. *Hand-Book of American Literature: Historical, Biographical and*

Critical. Port Washington, NY: Kennikat Press, 1856.

Harrington, Mark R. *Religion and Ceremonies of the Lenape.* Museum of the American Indian, Heye Foundation, Vol. 19, 1921.

Hearings before the Committee on Indian Affairs, in the Seventieth Congress, First and Second Session, 1926-1929. Washington: U.S. Government Printing Office, 1928.

Hearings on the Bill S. 2087, to Incorporate a Company for Breeding Horses on the Crow Indian Reservation, Montana and on the Bill S. 2963, for the Survey and Allotment of Indian Lands Within the Limits of the Crow Indian Reservation, Montana. 60th Congress, 1st Session, Senate Documents, Vol. 27, Doc. No. 445. Washington: U.S. Government Printing Office, 1908.

Hill, William. *The Agricultural and Hunting Methods of the Navaho Indians.* New Haven: Yale University Press, 1938.

Johnson, Broderick H. *Stories of Traditional Navajo Life and Culture.* Tsaile, AZ: Navajo Community College Press, 1977.

Jones, William. *Ethnography of the Fox Indians.* Smithsonian Institution, Bureau of American Ethnology, Bulletin 725. Washington: U.S. Government Printing Office, 1939.

Joseph, Chief. "An Indian's View of Indian Affairs". *North American Review*, No. 269, Vol. 128, April 1879.

Kip, Lawrence. *The Indian Council in the Valley of the Walla Walla.* 1855.

Kroeber, Alfred L. *Handbook of the Indians of California.* Smithsonian Institution, Bureau of American Ethnology, Bulletin 78. Washington: U.S. Government Printing Office, 1925.

La Flesche, Francis. *The Osage Tribe: Rite of the Wa-xo-be.* Smithsonian Institution, Bureau of American Ethnology, Forty-fifth Annual Report. Washington: U.S. Government Printing Office, 1930.

Lame Deer, John (Fire) & Erdoes, Richard. *Lame Deer: Seeker of Visions.* New York: Simon and Schuster, 1972.

Law, Jude. *The Colonial History of Vincennes, Under the French, British, and American Government.* Vincennes, IN: Harvey, Mason, 1858.

Leland, Charles G. *Algonquin Legends of New England; or, Myths and Folk Lore of the Micmac, Passamaquoddy, and Penobscot Tribes.* Boston: Houghton, Mifflin, 1884.

Linderman, Frank B. *Plenty Coups: Chief of the Crows*. Lincoln: University of Nebraska Press, 1930.

Lowie, Robert. "Studies in Plains Indian Folklore". *University of California Publications in American Archaeology and Ethnology*, Vol. 40, No. 1. Berkley: 1942.

MacEwan, Grant. *Tatanga-mani, Walking Buffalo of the Stonies*. Edmonton, Alberta: M.J. Hurtig, 1969.

Matthews, Washington (ed.). *Navajo Legends*. Boston: Houghton, Mifflin and Company, 1897.

———. *The Night Chant: A Navaho Ceremony*. Memoirs of the American Museum of Natural History, Whole Series Vol. 6, Anthropology Series Vol. 5. New York, 1902.

McClintock, Walter. *The Old North Trail: Or, Life, Legends and Religion of the Blackfeet Indians*. London: Macmillan & Co., 1910.

Miller, Jay (ed.). *Mourning Dove: A Salishan Autobiography*. Lincoln, NB: University of Nebraska Press, 1990.

Mooney, James. *Calendar History of the Kiowa Indians*. Smithsonian Institution, Bureau of American Ethnology, Seventeenth Annual Report, Pt.1. Washington: U.S. Government Printing Office, 1898.

———. *The Ghost-Dance Religion and the Sioux Outbreak of 1890*. Smithsonian Institution, Bureau of American Ethnology, Fourteenth Annual Report. Washington: U.S. Government Printing Office, 1896.

Morgan, Lewis H. *League of the Ho-dé-no-sau-nee, or Iroquois*. Rochester, NY: Sage & Brothers, 1851.

Neihardt, John G. (ed.). *Black Elk Speaks: Being the Life Story of a Holy Man of the Ogalala Sioux*. New York: William Morrow, 1932.

Parker, Arthur C. *The Constitution of the Five Nations, Or, The Iroquois Book of the Great Law*. New York State Museum, Bulletin 184. Albany: 1916.

Patterson, John B. (ed). *Life of Ma-ka-tai-me-she-kia-kiak, or Black Hawk*. Boston: Russell, Odiorne & Metcalf, 1834.

Petrone, Penny (ed.). *First People, First Voices*. Toronto: University of Toronto Press, 1991.

Qoyawayma, Polingaysi. *No Turning Back: A True Account of a Hopi Girl's Struggle to Bridge the Gap between the World of Her People and the World of the White Man.* Albuquerque: University of New Mexico Press, 1964.

Rasmussen, Knud. *The Intellectual Culture of the Iglulik Eskimos: Report of the Fifth Thule Expedition, 1921-24*, Vol. 7, No. 1. Copenhagen: Gyldendalske Boghandel, Nordisk Forlag, 1930.

Speck, Frank. "Native Tribes and Dialects of Connecticut: A Mohegan-Pequot Diary". In Smithsonian Institution, Bureau of American Ethnology, Forty-third Annual Report. Washington: U.S. Government Printing Office, 1903.

Spinden, Herbert Joseph. *Songs of the Tewa.* New York: Exposition of Indian Tribal Arts, 1933.

Standing Bear, Luther. *Land of the Spotted Eagle.* Boston: Houghton Mifflin, 1933.

———. *My Indian Boyhood.* Boston: Houghton Mifflin, 1931.

———. *Stories of the Sioux.* Boston: Houghton Mifflin, 1934.

Stands In Timber, John, & Liberty, Margot. *Cheyenne Memories.* New Haven: Yale University Press, 1967.

Stephen, Alexander. "Hopi Indians of Arizona". *The Masterkey*, January, Vol. 14. Los Angeles: Southwest Museum, 1940.

Tatham's Characters Among the North American Indians. London: Annual of Biography and Obituary, 1820.

Taylor, Nathaniel G., et al. *Papers Relating to Talks and Councils Held with the Indians in Dakota and Montana in the Years 1866-1869.* Washington: U.S. Government Printing Office, 1910.

Thalbitzer, William (ed.). *The Ammassalik Eskimo: Contributions to the Ethnology of the East Greenland Natives.* Copenhagen: Bianco Luno, 1923.

Thatcher, Benjamin. *Indian Biography, or, An Historical Account of Those Individuals who have been Distinguished among the North American Natives as Orators, Warriors, Statesmen, and other Remarkable Characters*, Vol. 2. New York: J. & J. Harper, 1832.

"The Report and Journal of Proceedings of the Commission Appointed to Obtain Certain Concessions from the Sioux Indians". In *The Annual Report of the Commissioner of Indian Affairs, 1876.* 44th Cong., 2nd sess., 1876-77, S. Exec. Doc. 9, (Serial 1718).

Turner, Frederick W., III (ed.). *The Portable North American Indian Reader.* New

York: Penguin Books, 1977.

Underhill Ruth M. *Red Man's Religion: Beliefs and Practices of the Indians North of Mexico.* Chicago: University of Chicago Press, 1965.

United States Congressional Serial Set, Vol. 2686. Washington: U.S. Government Printing Office, 1890.

Walker, James R., *The Sun Dance and Other Ceremonies of the Oglala Division of the Teton* Dakota. American Museum of Natural History, Anthropological Papers 16, Pt. 2. New York: 1917.

Walker, James. *Lakota Belief and Ritual*, eds. Raymond R. DeMallie & Elaine A. Jahner. Lincoln: University of Nebraska Press, 1991.

Warren, William W. "History of the Ojibways, Based upon Traditions and Oral Statements". In Minnesota Historical Society, Collection 5. St. Paul: Minnesota Historical Society, 1885.

Washburne, Heluiz C. *Land of the Good Shadows: The Life Story of Anauta, an Eskimo Woman.* New York: John Day, 1940.

Weatherly, Marina B. "Susie Walking Bear Yellowtail: A Life Story". *North Dakota Quarterly*, Vol. 67, No. 2, Spring, 2000.

Wheelwright, Mary C. (ed.). *Navajo Creation Myth: The Story of the Emergence.* Santa Fe: Museum of Navajo Ceremonial Art, 1942.

Wilson, Gilbert L. "Hidatsa Horse and Dog Culture." *Anthropological Papers of the American Museum of Natural History*, Vol. 15, Pt. 2. 1924.

———— (ed.). *Waheenee: An Indian Girls Story.* St. Paul: Webb Publishing, 1921.

Zitkala-Sa. "Why I Am a Pagan?" *Atlantic Monthly* 90, December 1902.

BIOGRAPHICAL NOTES

Michael Oren Fitzgerald is the author and editor of more than fifteen books that have received some two dozen awards, including the ForeWord Book of the Year Award, the Ben Franklin Award, and the USA Best Books Award. More than ten of Michael's books, along with two documentary films he produced, are used in high-school or university classes. He previously taught the Religious Traditions of the North American Indians at Indiana University. His works include *Indian Spirit, The Spirit of Indian Women, The Essential Charles Eastman,* and *Living in Two Worlds: The American Indian Experience.* Michael lives with his wife in Bloomington, Indiana.

Joseph A. Fitzgerald studied Comparative Religion at Indiana University, where he also earned a Doctor of Jurisprudence degree. A recipient of the Ben Franklin Award and numerous other awards, Joseph has edited ten books on diverse themes in world religion, culture, and philosophy. His works include *The Cheyenne Indians: Their History and Lifeways, Illustrated* and *World of the Teton Sioux Indians: Their Music, Life & Culture.* He lives with his wife and daughters in Bloomington, Indiana.

Joseph Bruchac is a world-renowned Native author and storyteller who has written more than 120 books for both children and adults. His work is heavily influenced by his Abenaki ancestry, and he has worked extensively with other family members on projects involving the preservation of Abenaki culture and language. His poems, articles, and stories have appeared in over 500 publications, including *National Geographic* and *Smithsonian Magazine.* Joseph's work has earned him numerous awards, including a Rockefeller Humanities Fellowship, a National Endowment for the Arts Writing Fellowship for Poetry, the Hope S. Dean Award for Notable Achievement in Children's Literature, and both the 1998 Writer of the Year Award and the 1998 Storyteller of the Year Award from the Wordcraft Circle of Native Writers and Storytellers. In 1999, he received the Lifetime Achievement Award from the Native Writers' Circle of the Americas. Joseph's most famous works include *Keepers of the Earth: Native American Stories and Environmental Activities for Children* (with Michael Caduto), *Code Talker: A Book About the Navajo Marines,* and *Crazy Horse's Vision* (illustrated by S.D. Nelson). He lives in Greenfield Center, New York.

World Wisdom's American Indian Titles

All Our Relatives: Traditional Native American Thoughts about Nature
compiled and illustrated by Paul Goble, 2005

The Boy and His Mud Horses: And Other Stories from the Tipi
compiled and illustrated by Paul Goble, 2010

The Cheyenne Indians: Their History and Lifeways
by George Bird Grinnell, edited by Joseph A. Fitzgerald, 2008

Children of the Tipi: Life in the Buffalo Days
edited by Michael Oren Fitzgerald, 2013

Custer's Last Battle: Red Hawk's Account of the Battle of the Little Bighorn
compiled and illustrated by Paul Goble, 2013

The Earth Made New: Plains Indian Stories of Creation
compiled and illustrated by Paul Goble, 2009

The Essential Charles Eastman (Ohiyesa)
edited by Michael Oren Fitzgerald, 2007

The Feathered Sun: Plains Indians in Art and Philosophy
by Frithjof Schuon, 1990

The Gospel of the Redman: Commemorative Edition
compiled by Ernest Thompson Seton and Julia M. Seton, 2005

Horse Raid: The Making of a Warrior
compiled and illustrated by Paul Goble, 2014

The Hunter's Promise
by Joseph Bruchac, illustrated by Bill Farnsworth, 2015

The Image Taker: The Selected Stories and Photographs of Edward S. Curtis
edited by Gerald Hasuman and Bob Kapoun, 2009

Indian Spirit: Revised and Enlarged
edited by Judith and Michael Oren Fitzgerald, 2006

Living in Two Worlds: The American Indian Experience
by Charles Eastman, edited by Michael Oren Fitzgerald, 2010

The Man Who Dreamed of Elk-Dogs: & Other Stories from the Tipi
compiled and illustrated by Paul Goble, 2012

Native Spirit: The Sun Dance Way
by Thomas Yellowtail, edited by Michael Oren Fitzgerald, 2007

The Otter, the Spotted Frog, and the Great Flood
by Gerald Hausman, illustrated by Ramon Shiloh, 2013

Red Cloud's War: Brave Eagle's Account of the Fetterman Fight
compiled and illustrated by Paul Goble, 2015

The Spirit of Indian Women
edited by Judith and Michael Oren Fitzgerald, 2005

Spirit of the Earth: Indian Voices on Nature
edited by Joseph and Michael Oren Fitzgerald, 2017

*The Spiritual Legacy of the American Indian: Commemorative Edition
with Letters While Living with Black Elk*
by Joseph Epes Brown, 2007

The Thunder Egg
by Tim Myers, illustrated by Winfield Coleman, 2015

Tipi: Home of the Nomadic Buffalo Hunters
compiled and illustrated by Paul Goble, 2007

Whispers of the Wolf
by Pauline Ts'o, 2015

The Women who Lived with Wolves: And Other Stories from the Tipi
compiled and illustrated by Paul Goble, 2011

World of the Teton Sioux Indians: Their Music, Life & Culture
by Frances Densmore, edited by Joseph A. Fitzgerald, 2016

Films about American Indian Spirituality

Native Spirit & The Sun Dance Way
produced by Michael Oren Fitzgerald, directed by Jennifer Casey, 2007